ACPL ITE ✓ SO-EMF-067

DISCARDED

About this book

If you had grown up in a Saxon village a thousand years ago, life would have been very tough indeed, unless your family was rich. Children had to help with the farming — and the fighting. There was no school, except for the sons of nobles and for boys who wanted to become monks. But there was the fun of feast days, with minstrels playing in the big hall and lots to eat and drink.

The Saxons were people from Holland, Denmark and Germany who settled in England in the fifth century AD. They flourished for 600 years between the departure of the Romans and the arrival of the Norman conquerors in 1066. At first they believed in their fierce gods of war and thunder. Later on they became Christians. Alfred the Great was the most famous Saxon king. He made the laws fairer for everyone, as well as fighting off the Viking invaders who sailed across the sea in their long-ships. As you will see from the pictures in this book, Saxon children had hard but exciting lives.

Growing up in a Saxon Village

AMANDA PURVES

Wayland

ALLEN COUNTY PUBLIC LIBRARY
FORT WAYNE, INDIANA

Growing up in Other Times

Growing up in Ancient Rome
Amanda Purves

Growing up in Ancient Greece
Amanda Purves

Growing up in a Saxon Village
Amanda Purves

Growing up with the Vikings
Amanda Purves

Growing up with the Red Indians
Ann Palmer

Growing up with the Highland Clans
Raymond Lamont Brown

Growing up in Colonial America
Ann Palmer

Frontispiece: A Saxon family

ISBN 0 85340 543 3
Copyright © 1978 by Wayland Publishers Ltd
First published in 1978 by Wayland Publishers Ltd
49 Lansdowne Place, Hove, East Sussex, BN3 1HF, England
Text set in 12 pt. VIP Univers by Trident Graphics Ltd, Reigate
Printed in Great Britain by Gale and Polden Ltd, Aldershot, and
bound by The Pitman Press Ltd, Bath

Contents

7009428

1. The Family

The family was very important to Saxons. They called it the kindred. Fathers, mothers, children, uncles, aunts and grandparents all lived together like a tribe. Everyone, including the old, sick and unmarried, was cared for and loved. If a member of the family was killed, the murderer had to pay money to the family. If the murderer refused to pay, there was a blood feud. This meant hunting out and killing the murderer or one of his family. The Saxons also valued friendship and loyalty. They believed that betrayal was the worst crime of all.

The men treated women as equals. This was unusual at that time in history. And parents were kind to their children but very firm. Boys were expected to be brave and good fighters. Girls had to be good housekeepers and wives. They married when they were little more than children. The marriages were arranged by their parents, but no-one was forced to marry someone he or she really hated.

Life was much shorter as the Saxons did not know how to prevent or cure diseases. Most people died before they were forty but we know that a few lived to be over eighty.

Birth The Saxons didn't have hospitals, so a mother gave birth to her baby at home. She was helped by friends and relatives. The baby was wrapped in a blanket and shown to the father, who had to claim the baby as his own. Boys were given names like Ethelred and Egbert. A girl might be called Aegifu or Hilda.

Clothes Boys wore the same style of clothes as their fathers. These three Saxons are wearing woolen tunics and cloaks. The boy on the right is *cross-gartered.* This means he is wearing leather strips over woolen trousers to keep his legs warm. Girls wore woolen dresses over tunics. This noble lady's dress is embroidered. If you look at the other pictures in this book you will see that most women wore mantles (cloaks with hoods to cover their hair). In the summer few people wore shoes. In the winter leather shoes were worn.

This woman has just given birth to a baby and is showing it to the father for his approval.

Jewellery Men, women and children all wore as much jewellery as they could afford. Some wore little necklaces like this one, made out of painted clay beads. Others wore brooches. The big one here is called the Fuller Brooch. It shows the five senses — sight, smell, hearing, taste and touch. Women wore chatelaines around their waists as a mark of importance. They hung their household keys and knives on them.

Marriage There were two parts to a Saxon marriage ceremony. First there was the pledging, when the bride price was paid. Later the bride was given in marriage and the feasting began. Girls usually married when they were only twelve and boys when they were fifteen.

13

d pe`hi ferre l' fiide q̃ se iiilia pauitr. Herba dracni cũ Aceto ipofita pfectiffime

Nomen herbe. Cyclaminos. Omoeos. Celeron.
Alii. Anaion. Alii. Caffofillos. Alii. Chedomen. Zor
aftis. Chachena. Alii. Sampauer. dicunt. Alii. Boftam

Medicine Most Saxons prayed to their gods when they were ill. They also put leeches on their arms. The leeches sucked out the blood and the Saxons hoped they would suck out the disease at the same time. Sometimes they took medicine made from herbs, as you can see in these pictures.

Death The Saxons believed in life after death, so when they were buried some of their possessions were put in the grave with them. These beautiful gold clasps were found in a chief's ship grave at Sutton Hoo, Suffolk. Although the ship had rotted, there were all sorts of jewelled and gold treasures — a helmet, a shield, swords, a harp, a whetstone and brooches. But no body! Perhaps the ship was buried as a memorial to a chief who had been swept away in a river after a battle and whose body had never been found.

16

The picture on the facing page shows the ship-burial at Sutton Hoo, discovered in 1939. The pictures above and below are details from the beautiful gold clasps that were found in the grave.

2. Life at Home

Saxons lived in isolated farms, in small villages and, later on, in towns. Many English villages still have their Saxon names. Wickham, Comberton and Ingatestone, for instance. In fact any name which has "ton", "wick", "ing" or "ham" in it was probably once a Saxon village.

In a typical village, little huts clustered around the hall of the thegn. The hall was the biggest building. There was a pond, common land for grazing animals, and fields for growing crops. A fence was built round the village to keep out wolves and unfriendly neighbours. The ceorls (farm workers) all worked for the thegn, who protected them in times of danger.

Villagers grew all their own food and made almost everything they needed themselves. It was a full-time job for everyone, children included. The answer to this riddle is one of the most important things the Saxons made:

"I'm told a certain object grew
In the corner, rose and expanded and threw up
A crust! A proud wife carried off
That boneless wonder, the daughter of a king
Covered that swollen thing with a cloth."

Houses A ceorl's house was little more than a wooden hut covered in thatch. There were no windows, just a hole in the roof for a chimney. The door was an open space which was covered at night by a piece of animal skin. It must have been very dark, smoky and smelly. Even the richest men's houses were lit by candles or lights made out of rushes. The mother of King Ethelred II once beat him with candles, with the result that he hated candles for the rest of his life.

Halls Early thegns lived in halls built of logs with thatched roofs. Later, halls were made of stone with tiny windows called eye-slits. Inside, shields and tapestries decorated the walls. Rushes spread on the floor made a sort of carpet. They weren't changed very often so they must have smelled rather nasty! There were tables and benches round the big log fire where all the food was cooked. At night "benches were pushed back, the floor was padded with beds and pillows," says the poem *Beowulf.*

Pottery Skilled potters made pots by hand until the eighth century. Then potters' wheels made their work much easier. Saxons used pots for all sorts of things — as jugs and burial urns, and for storing oils and grains. Sometimes these were made out of metals such as bronze by the smiths. They lasted longer than the earthenware ones but only wealthy families could afford them. Some pots were decorative as well as useful.

Glass Saxon glass was very beautiful. Unlike our own clear glass, it was shades of purple, blue and green. As you can see, some of the glasses were very ornate. The glass in the middle is called a tumbler. It tumbles over when it is put down. The idea was to drink the contents in one gulp and never put it down!

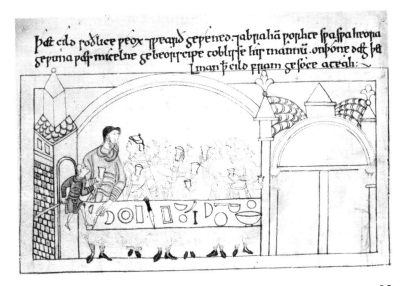

Food Porridge, cheese, wayside weeds, barley cakes, wild berries and fruit — these are the foods the Saxons usually ate. Not very exciting. They rarely ate meat, except at feasts. There was no sugar, so food had to be sweetened with honey. Their favourite drink, mead, was made from honey, too. Honey was so valuable that Saxons sometimes paid the rent with it. They kept bees in wicker hives like this one. Ordinary families ate off hunks of bread or wooden platters. Only kings had lovely spoons like these from Sutton Hoo.

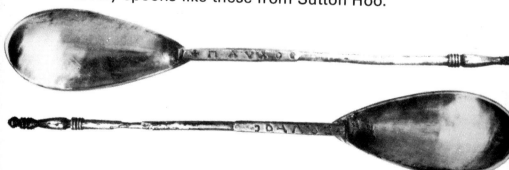

Weaving Saxon girls and women were expert weavers. They made all the family's clothes and blankets. First the wool was combed, then it was

24

made into yarn and woven on a loom. The looms were upright like this and weights were used to keep them from wobbling. The cloth was dyed with vegetable and plant dyes.

Furniture Most homes had very little furniture – perhaps just a few stools and a blanket chest to keep bedding and clothes in. Royalty did a little better. Here you can see a king lounging in a rather pretty four-poster bed. Most people slept on the floor or on benches.

imago leonis

ÓAGI
HA
R

US
CUS

3. School and Court

Very few Saxons could read or write — there was no need to in everyday life. And very few children went to school. There were some schools for boys who wanted to become monks, or for the sons of noblemen. Most children were taught by their parents. Girls learned how to be good house-wives, and boys how to be skilful farmers and fighting men.

It was the duty of the kings to make up the laws, and everyone had to obey them. If they didn't, there were horrible punishments such as chop-ping off hands and ears. Children were punished just as severely as adults if they broke the law. Most laws said that if someone harmed you, he either paid you compensation or you hurt him back! There was no police force, so every man and boy in the village had to make sure everyone was behaving. If a person did something wrong, the whole village chased after him until he was caught. Sometimes a hunted man hid and became an outlaw. If he managed to reach a church he could be given sanctuary, which meant that no-one could touch him.

We may feel that some of their punishments were very cruel but Saxons tried to be fair — and not many people broke the law.

Schools Monks set up monastery schools to teach boys how to become monks themselves. Boys started school when they were very young. One boy called Esica was only three! They learned reading, writing, poetry, astronomy, Greek and Latin. Palace schools (also called noble schools) were begun in the ninth century by King Alfred. They were schools for princes and the sons of noblemen to learn reading and writing in Anglo-Saxon and Latin, hunting, wrestling and music.

Saxons wrote with styli such as these, made out of metal or bone and dipped in ink. They wrote on vellum, which is made out of dried and stretched animal skins. Here are two examples of their writing. On the left is part of a Bible written in Latin. On the right is a Saxon account of one of King Alfred's victories in battle.

Justice The picture shows a Saxon king and his council holding a court of law. But most people settled their own differences. Everybody had a price for his or her life, called the wergild. A thegn was worth 1,200 shillings, a ceorl 200. If someone was killed or injured, the slayer had to pay the wergild to the dead person's family. Otherwise the family could take revenge.

Trials Sometimes if there was no evidence an accused person was tried by ordeal. First he had to drink a cup of holy water. Then he might be tied up and thrown into a pond or stream. If he sank he was innocent, but if he floated he was guilty! King Alfred decided to make trials fairer by having a jury, made up of people who didn't know the accused person or his accuser. The picture below shows Alfred presiding over a trial. The twelve people in the background are the jury.

Bootless Crimes Crimes that were punishable by death were called bootless crimes. They included disloyalty to the king, murder and setting fire to houses. Hanging was the most common form of execution. Occasionally, if the court was feeling merciful, the guilty person had their ears or hands cut off instead!

4. Work and Play

The Saxons had to work very hard most of the time. Their main concern was to grow enough food to live on. The farmers' year followed a pattern of ploughing, sowing and harvesting. Many of the pictures in this chapter show you the different tasks set for each month. They come from an old calender. Opposite you can see that in May they watched sheep, in June cut wood, in July it was haymaking time and in November they are standing around a fire. Children helped with much of the work, especially looking after animals.

As well as growing food, Saxons made jewellery and ornaments and traded with other countries. Smiths and merchants were important people in Saxon towns and villages.

We don't know very much about children's games. Tiny swords and axes have been found, so they certainly played soldiers. Like their parents, they probably enjoyed feast days best of all. There was plenty to eat and drink then, and musicians and dancers provided lively entertainment. The Yule feast in December was the biggest and longest of the year. But for most of the time life consisted of going to bed early, getting up at dawn and working on the land all day.

God spede þe plouȝ: & sende us korne I nolt

Farmers Saxons ploughed their fields in narrow strips. Even women and children helped. One ploughman said he had a boy "to urge on the oxen with a goad; he is now hoarse on account of the cold and his shouting". Once the crop was ripe, farmers used sickles to cut the corn. Later, they beat the corn to separate the grain. It was often ground into flour by hand.

Farm Animals Oxen usually pulled the ploughs and carts. Sometimes asses were used instead. Oxen and horses were the Saxons' most valuable farm animals. An ox was worth 30 pieces of silver, a horse cost half a pound of silver, a pig was tenpence, and a sheep could be bought for fourpence. Animals were smaller than today's and were usually looked after by children.

A Saxon farmyard – the animals were usually looked after by the children.

Ploughing and harrowing on a Saxon farm — the boys and young men are helping with the work.

Smiths Metal was used for many things, especially for weapons, farm implements and pots. Ordinary smiths were kept busy. There were also goldsmiths and silversmiths who made jewellery

and ornaments for the rich. This carving, made on whalebone about 700 AD, shows Wayland the Smith at work. In legend, Wayland was a sea-giant's son who made a feathered robe and flew!

Merchants Saxon merchants often travelled overseas to buy and sell, and pedlars went from village to village to trade. This is what one merchant had for sale: "Purple garments and silks; precious gems and gold; strange raiment and spices, wine and oil; ivory and brass; copper and tin; sulphur and glass, and many such things."

Money At first, the Saxons had no money. They used bars of silver or other metals. When trade with other countries became important about 700, they found they needed real money. They had pennies and sixpences made of silver or gold. Later, there were pounds (worth 240 pennies) and shillings (48 or 60 to the pound). These are some of the many different Saxon coins which have been found.

Hunting and Hawking Deer, boars and hares were hunted for food and for fun. As you can see on page 48, for a boar hunt, Saxons used dogs and hunting horns. Hawking was the sport of kings and noble people. They trained wild hawks to kill other small birds and kept them as pets. Ceorls simply shot birds with their bows and arrows.

Feasts Everyone enjoyed the feasts held in the thegn's hall, especially the Yule feast in December. The thegn, his family and warriors sat at the high table. The ceorls sat lower down and women had a table of their own. Children and dogs sat on the floor! There was lots to eat – roast boar and stuffed eels, for instance – and even more to drink.

Hunting in Saxon England. The picture above shows two Saxon men hawking. The exotic bird on the right looks like as ostrich.

The picture below is taken from an eleventh-century calender. The strange creatures on the right are wild boar which once roamed England.

After the hunting came the feasting. These Saxons are settling down to a meal of wild boar with lots of wine thrown in.

Entertainment After the feast, and often between courses as well, there was the entertainment. Sometimes it was dancing, sometimes it

was singing. Minstrels provided the music on strange instruments like these. Harps and lyres were popular too.

54

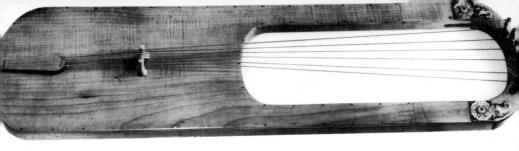

The picture on the facing page shows a man playing an early voilin. The picture above is of a Saxon
lyre while the man below is playing a set of simple
bagpipes.

5. One God or Many?

The first Saxons who settled in Britain believed in hundreds of gods. Their chief god was Woden. Other important ones were Tiw, the god of war; Thunor, the god of thunder; Frig, the goddess of love; and Erce, the mother of the earth. They named days of the week after their gods. Wednesday meant Woden's Day, Tuesday was Tiw's Day, and so on. Even our word Easter comes from a goddess called Eostre. The Saxons were very superstitious and believed in all kinds of spells and magic. They worshipped in the open air so that evil spirits couldn't harm them! And to keep their gods happy, they made sacrifices to them.

During the fifth century, missionaries were sent from Rome and Ireland to convert the Saxons to Christianity. This was a very hard job as the old gods were popular. But by the end of the seventh century Woden and all the others had few supporters. The Saxons built churches of wood and stone, some of which are still standing today. Many Saxons became monks, living simple lives and copying out the Bible by hand. Few people apart from monks could read or write. They were good artists too, and we can still see some of their illustrated manuscripts today.

Old Gods The Saxon gods were mostly fierce and warlike. This is Thunor, the god of thunder. Worshippers made them sacrifices. Sometimes the sacrifices were little honey cakes, but more often animals and even humans were killed and offered to them. It was very important to keep the gods in a good mood! But to get to Valhalla, the Saxon heaven, it was necessary to die a violent death — preferably in battle. Once there, people believed they would spend all their time eating and drinking and listening to stories about brave warriors and the battles they fought in.

Runes The letters of the old Saxon alphabet were called runes. They were thought to have magical powers. Runes could be used to curse enemies — but they believed that spells sometimes backfired! This sword is carved with runes for good luck in battle. And there are runes round the sides of this precious casket, even though the rest of the carving tells the Christian story of the three wise men bringing gifts to the baby Jesus.

Christianity St Augustine saw some Anglo-Saxon children in the slave market at Rome and exclaimed that they were "Angels not Angles". The Pope sent him to England to convert all the

Saxons to Christianity. He was welcomed by King Ethelbert, who became a Christian himself. Other missionaries sailed across the sea from Ireland or from other parts of Europe to convert the Saxons.

St Augustine baptising King Ethelbert.

A Saxon bishop carrying his gospel book.

Monks This picture shows a monk being tonsured – having his hair specially cut. Monks also had to wear special clothes called habits. They promised to leave behind their possessions and

families and live simply in the monastery, helping
with the cooking, gardening and farming as well
as praying. The picture above shows St Guthlac, a
seventh-century monk.

Lindisfarne A monk called Aidan built one of the first English monasteries at Lindisfarne, a small island off the coast of Northumbria, in 634. This is what it looks like today. The monks at Lin-

disfarne copied and illustrated the first four books
of the New Testament. You can see the Lindisfarne Gospels in the British Library, where they
glow with colour. Overleaf are two Gospel pages.

68

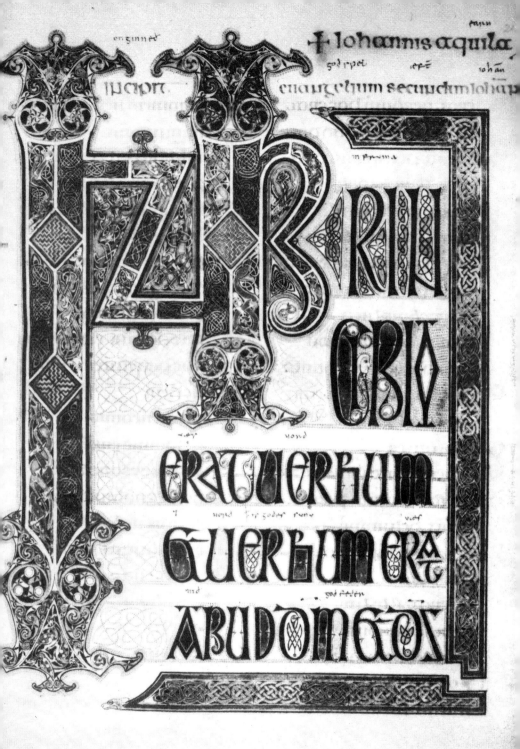

69

Churches Saxon churches were very small. The early ones were made out of wood, like the church at Greensted (on next page). Later on they were made of stone, like this church at Bradford-on-Avon (left). Inside they were brightly painted with pictures of stories from the Bible. In lonely spots where there were no churches, people gathered around a wooden or stone cross to listen to the monks.

The wooden, Saxon church at Greensted in Essex.

6. Warriors

The Saxons had to do a lot of fighting. They had to fight the Britons before they could settle in the fifth century and make Britain their home. Then they fought amongst themselves for important positions and power. But the most ferocious enemy they had to deal with was the Vikings.

The Vikings came across the North Sea from Scandinavia. In 793 they attacked the monastery at Lindisfarne – a year when strange flashes of lightning and fiery dragons were supposedly seen in the sky! After that, the attacks continued until the Vikings controlled most of England. The only bit they couldn't conquer was the Kingdom of Wessex, where the famous King Alfred put up a heroic defence. But in the eleventh century when the Vikings attacked again, there was no such brave leader and England was ruled by a Viking – King Cnut.

The Saxons were good fighters. Boys were taught how to use weapons by their fathers. We even hear of women and girls fighting. In time of war every healthy man had to fight in a force, which was called the fyrd. The last people the Saxons fought were the Normans in 1066. I think we all know the result of that battle!

Warriors Spearmen, swordsmen and archers were the main sorts of fighters in Saxon times. As you can see from the pictures, most of them wore their ordinary clothes to battle. Few men wore armour, and the archer leading the group of spearmen doesn't even have shoes on. The warriors were mostly part-time fighters. In time of peace they went home to their families to tend their crops and animals.

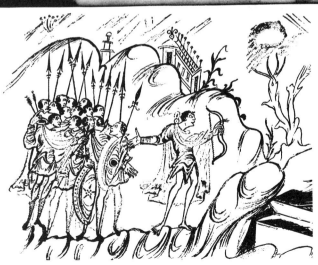

78

Weapons The Saxons fought with a variety of weapons. Here are some of them – an axe and spearheads. There were also swords and bows and arrows. Some warriors carried shields made out of wood with a metal boss in the middle. This shield has beautiful decorations. At the bottom is a winged dragon of gilt-bronze. The ornaments were found at Sutton Hoo and the shield has been reconstructed.

Swords This sword was found at Abingdon, near to one of Alfred the Great's battlegrounds. Swords were treasured and handed down from father to son. In the eleventh century Prince Aethelstan still had a sword which had belonged to his ancestor Offa (above) three hundred years before. Swords were often carved and some even had names!

81

Whetstones Before soldiers went into battle they sharpened their spears and swords on whetstones. This one, found at Sutton Hoo, was probably used only for show in some sort of ceremony. It is very big — this is only a part of it. The faces carved on it were perhaps part of a magic spell to bring good luck in battle.

Helmets Only wealthy soldiers could afford to have helmets. This magnificent one belonged to the unknown king or chief buried at Sutton Hoo. It is made out of iron and has a nose, mouth, moustache and eyebrows of bronze. Inside it is padded with scraps of wool and leather, like the crash helmets that motor cyclists wear today.

Sailors The Saxons were good sailors. Their fighting ships were narrow and swift. King Alfred designed his own ships, which were paid for out

of taxes. Sailors who could "boldly drive the ship across the salt sea" were much respected. This ship is carrying the Saxon King Harold.

Vikings The Vikings came from Norway, Sweden and Denmark. Like the Saxons, they wanted to conquer Britain and settle down to farm. They

were fierce warriors and great sailors. The Saxons fought battles against the Vikings for over two hundred years. They didn't always win!

Normans The Saxons' last enemy was the Normans. In 1066 they fought hard against the Norman invaders at the Battle of Hastings. The story of this famous battle is told in the Bayeux Tapestry. This Norman embroidery is about 80 m

ET FRANCI: INPRELIO

(230 ft) long. According to legend it was made by William the Conqueror's wife Matilda. As you can see from these scenes from the tapestry, the Saxons fought hard. But they lost, William was crowned king and Saxon England came to an end.

New Words

Bootless crime A crime for which there was no compensation. The punishment was usually death by hanging. Murder, disloyalty to the king, and setting fire to property were bootless crimes.

Ceorl An ordinary Saxon, not a nobleman.

Cross-garters Leather strips would round the legs.

Fyrd The main Saxon fighting force in times of war. Most of its members were ceorls who were not trained soldiers. They looked after their land unless there was an emergency.

Pledging The Saxon engagement to be married.

Runes The letters of the early Saxon alphabet. They were often used as magic signs.

Thegn A Saxon chief.

Valhalla The Saxon heaven for those who died violently.

Wergild The price of a life in Saxon times. It was higher for a nobleman than for an ordinary man. It had to be paid as compensation to a slain person's family.

More Books

A Saxon Settler by R Sutcliff (Oxford University Press, 1965). A lively description of a Saxon family's life. Suitable for older readers.

Everyday Life in Roman and Anglo-Saxon Times by M and C H B Quennell (Batsford, 1959; Carousel, 1972). Packed full of detail and interesting stories. For advanced readers.

From Cavemen to Vikings by R J Unstead (Black, 1953; Carousel, 1975). A useful book for younger readers. All aspects of Saxon life clearly shown and explained.

Saxons and Saints by A Watson (Chambers, 1976). A very good account of the Saxons' conversion to Christianity.

Saxons and Vikings by G Middleton (Longman, 1968). An excellent book, full of well-presented pictures and information.

Wordhoard by G Paton Walsh and K Crossley-Holland (Macmillan, 1969; Puffin, 1972). Excellent stories about the Saxons. Suitable for older readers.

Index

Picture Credits

The author and publishers would like to thank all those who have given permission for copyright pictures to be reproduced on the following pages: The Trustees of the British Museum, 12 *top,* 13, 15, 16, 17 *top and bottom,* 23 *bottom,* 24 *bottom,* 26, 29 *top left and top right,* 36 *bottom,* 45 48–49 *top and bottom,* 55 *top,* 58 *bottom,* 64, 65, 68, 69, 76–77, 78 *top and bottom,* 82, 83; Leicester Museum, *frontispiece;* The Bodleian Library, 6, 10–11, 32; Radio Times and Hulton Picture Library, 14; The Mansell Collection, 21 *top,* 30, 56, 58 *top,* 60–61, 84–85; Museum of London, 22 *left and right,* 79; Peter Clayton, 24 *top;* Mary Evans Picture Library, 28, 38–39, 40–41, 62; County Council of Essex Education Department, 72–73; A F Kersting, 70; Ashmoleam Museum, 81; Department of the Environment, Crown Copyright 66–67, 86–87; Giraudon, 88–89, 90–91. The remaining pictures belong to the Wayland Picture Library.